MORE

of

Jesus

LESS OF ME

Principles for Fruitful Living

Printed in the United States of America

Published in Hellertown, PA

Library of Congress Control Number 2020908936
ISBN 978-1-950459-03-2
2 4 6 8 10 9 7 5 3 1 paperback

MomosaPublishing.com

ENDORSEMENT

Whether sharing her heart within the pages of a book or sharing a message front and center at a conference event, Jessie Seneca is passionate and girlfriend-real to encourage women to find MORE OF JESUS! Filled with rich Biblical truths and helpful principles, this little book will challenge and inspire you to find fruitful living and a deeper relationship with Jesus.

—VERNA BOWMAN, SPEAKER AND AUTHOR OF
CRUMBS ALONG THE BROKEN PATH AND *GATHERING*

This book is dedicated to the One
who made More of Him Ministries possible
and attainable. I am forever grateful for
the calling God put on my life and the dream
He set in my heart through every success,
heartbreak, and opportunity. And to those who
have walked the journey of ministry with me—
you rock! Together, we celebrate 10 years
of ministry. I can't wait to see what the
next 10 years will bring.

*"Let us not lose heart in doing good,
for in due time we will reap
if we do not grow weary."*
GALATIANS 6:9

CONTENTS

CHAPTER ONE
More of Jesus
7

CHAPTER TWO
Less of Me
30

CHAPTER THREE
Principles for Fruitful Living
52

EPILOGUE
Christ in Your Heart
78

Endnotes
81

About the Author
82

MORE OF JESUS

**"He must become greater;
I must become less."**
JOHN 3:30 (NIV)

I took one of the greatest (and scariest) leaps in my life in 2010 when I stepped away from a loved ministry I served for nearly nine years to begin the ministry God had called me to more than 14 years earlier. I remember the day so vividly. It meant leaving behind co-laborers and familiarity and facing many days of solitude and uncertainty as I transitioned to working in my quiet home.

I sat in my new office space with my new coworkers, Bella and Murphy, the furry golden-doodles, staring at a blank chalkboard with plenty of thoughts running through my head.

It was time to name the ministry God ordained and prepared beforehand.

While reading through the Book of John, the words leaped off the page as I read John 3:30, "He must become greater; I must become less." There it was: More of Him.

> More of Him.
> More of Him . . . Less of me.
> More of Him Ministries.

This is such a short verse, yet it is filled with big meaning. Much reflection of this verse over the years has impacted my days and convicted my walk in ways I never imagined possible. Together, we will unfold what it means to set our selfish desires aside in order to more deeply desire God and pursue a faith-centered lifestyle—one fully devoted to Him. Surely, this is not an easy task, and it's a battle I fight as well, but it's a desire worth seeking and searching for until the end of our days.

What Does It Mean to Have More of Jesus?

Let's learn this lesson from John 3:26-30 (NIV).

> They came to John and said to him, "Rabbi, that man who was with you on the other side of the Jordan—the one you testified about—look, he is baptizing, and everyone is going to him." To this John replied, "A person can receive only what is given them from heaven. You yourselves can testify that I said, 'I am not the Messiah but am sent ahead of him.' The bride belongs to the bridegroom. The friend who attends the bridegroom waits and listens for him, and is full of joy when he hears the bridegroom's voice. That joy is mine, and it is now complete. He must become greater; I must become less.

The Book of John captures an incredible conversation between John the Baptist and his disciples talking about Jesus and the start of His ministry. John knew his place in God's story, so much so that when Jesus showed up to be baptized by him, John told Jesus that it should be the other way around—that John should be baptized by Jesus (Matthew 3:14).

Yes, John knew his place, and it wasn't first. John had to make room for God to move in with His indescribable gift—Jesus (2 Corinthians 9:15).

The *selfie*-centered lifestyle that we have come to socially accept is putting us at the center of everything. This is the opposite of what God desires. He wants to be at the center of your life. Rather than asking, "what is in it for me?" we should ask, "what will bring God the greatest glory?" Just as John lowered himself so that Jesus could be elevated, we must do the same. Put Jesus first!

John 3:30 practically teaches us how to look at our intentions and ask the question, "Am I doing this for my glory, or am I doing this for God's glory?"

If your answer isn't the latter, your prayer should be for God to come and change your heart. If God isn't the one receiving the glory, then we must check the motive behind the decision or action and make an adjustment. He must increase, and we must decrease.

For Jesus to increase, you may need to receive Him as Lord, make a commitment to meet with God on a daily basis, or expand that meeting time by 10 minutes. It might be that you commit to read through the Bible in a year, memorize a certain number of Scriptures, begin a Bible study with friends, surrender a decision, or commit to practicing what you read in your daily life. Making God a priority will always include some kind of sacrifice on your part. For each of us, it looks a little different, but the common threads should be to walk closer with Him, live more deliberately for Him, and desire more of Him. The more territory we allow Christ to occupy in our hearts, the more effective His influence will be on what we say and do.

Because Christ died for us, we should no longer desire to live for ourselves, but for Him who died and rose again on our behalf (2 Corinthians 5:15).

PRINCIPLES FOR MORE OF JESUS

PRINCIPLE #1
Abide in Him

"Abide in Me, and I in you. As the branch cannot bear fruit of itself unless it abides in the vine, so neither can you unless you abide in Me."

JOHN 15:4

We have to invite Him into our daily lives and we must choose to abide in Him. We have to ask for more of Him. John 15:4-5 says, "Abide in Me, and I in you. As the branch cannot bear fruit of itself unless it abides in the vine, so neither can you unless you abide in Me. I am the vine, you are the branches; he who abides in Me and I in Him, he bears much fruit, for apart from Me you can do nothing."

In Greek, abide (menō) means "to dwell, continue, tarry, or endure."[1] All of these verbs have a common denominator—to remain for a period of time. When you and I long to be in God's Word for any length of time, we will be captured by His presence. Psalm 91:1 in the NKJV, says, "He who dwells in the secret place of the Most High shall abide under the shadow of the Almighty." When you learn to dwell in the secret place of the Most High, you are putting yourself in a position to discover the key to true Kingdom fruitfulness. The secret place is central to overcoming life, and one of the best kept secrets of our faith is the blessedness and joy of cultivating this secret life with God.[2] Spending time in the secret place with God is for our own good.

In His presence, you will find a place of safety and rest that sweeps over you, and you will never be the same. May we profess the very words David proclaimed in Psalm 62:1a (CSB), "I am at rest in God alone." Again, this will require sacrifice, the choice to be still, and the vigilance to keep the clutter in your life from overshadowing the necessity of living close to God. His Word tells us in 1 John 2:6, "the one who says he abides in Him ought himself to walk in the same manner as He walked." Our abiding should impact the way we live out our days.

We find a great, although unconventional, visual of this concept in the movie *City Slickers*. In this film, each year three friends vacation away from their wives. One trip finds them on a midlife crisis adventure through a cattle drive across the Southwest. On their journey, their cowboy guide, Curly, gets into a deep conversation with one of the friends, Mitch. The two talk about the meaning of life. Holding up one finger, Curly shares how there is *one thing* in life, and it's up to each of us to find out what that one purpose is. As their trip continues, the movie reveals that Mitch finds the true meaning of life, for him, in a raging river, saving a baby calf.

Can't we relate? Don't we each desire to understand truly what our purpose in life is? Thankfully, as believers in Jesus Christ, that purpose is crystal clear—to know Jesus.

When you have Christ, you have everything. He is your life (Colossians 3:4).

He is the *one thing* that satisfies, but you must seek Him. David declared this in Psalm 27:4, "One thing I have asked from the Lord, that I shall seek: that I may dwell in the house of the Lord all the days of my life, to behold the beauty of the Lord and to meditate in His temple."

This Scripture captures the heart and passion of David. Although he spent countless hours tending his father's sheep and running from King Saul, he never lost the desire for the presence of the Lord. From the pasture to the strongholds of the wilderness, his deepest longing was to be near to God—nestled in the secret place.

May we pursue this *one thing*—to seek Him above ourselves. By dwelling in His presence, beholding His beauty, and meditating on His Word, we'll find ourselves walking our faith journey toward this truth and unlocking principles to a fruitful and empowered life.

Draw Near to God

"The Lord is near to all who call upon Him, to all who call upon Him in truth."

PSALM 145:18

What do you have to do to be near to God? Call on Him. Talk with Him. That's it. The nearness of God is as close as you make it. The Lord is near to *ALL* who call on Him. Just as Asaph, a minister of music in the temple, concluded in Psalm 73:28, "But as for me, the nearness of God is my good; I have made the Lord God my refuge, that I may tell of all Your works." So, you and I must understand the importance of being close to God. It changes everything.

Sometimes we complicate what it looks like to be close to God when all He asks of us is to call on Him. I have heard it expressed this way, "The Lord is as near to you as a prayer."

You might feel that God is far away, but all you have to do is call His name and begin to pray, and that sense of His distance vanishes. You will come into a living encounter with God. He is a God who is near, not a far off God (Jeremiah 23:23). There are no exceptions. He will disclose Himself to those who love Him (John 14:21). Look no further than the moment you're in for the nearness of God, and His presence will go with you throughout your day. In 1 Kings 19, Elijah was running for his life out of fear due to the threat Jezebel made—to eliminate him. As Elijah met with God, it wasn't through a strong wind, a great earthquake, or a blazing fire where he heard from Him. It was in a gentle whisper that God spoke (1 Kings 19:12).

Too many times we look to hear from God in big and magnificent ways, and we miss Him in the stillness of the ordinary. Often, we want to think that God gives us signs, and perhaps He does. But it's in your daily meeting with God, through the pages of His Scriptures, where He will come alive to you. As Jesus rode into Jerusalem and taught in the temple, Luke 19:48 declares, "...for all the people were hanging on to every word He said." Does this reflect our attitude when we read His Word? For His Word is transforming, cleansing, and will equip you when you seek Him. We can cling to His promise that He draws near to those who draw near to Him (James 4:8).

PRINCIPLE # 3
Behold Him

**"One thing I have asked from the Lord,
that I shall seek: that I may dwell in the
house of the Lord all the days of my life,
to behold the beauty of the Lord
and to meditate in His temple."**

PSALM 27:4

In the New Testament, Paul similarly says in
2 Corinthians 3:18, "But we all, with unveiled
face, beholding as in a mirror the glory of the
Lord, are being transformed into the same
image from glory to glory, just as from the
Lord, the Spirit."

You and I become whatever and whoever
we behold. So, where we spend our time and
who we spend our time with are important.

In 2 Corinthians 3, Paul builds on Moses'
experience after he spent 40 days and 40
nights on Mt. Sinai with God. When Moses
came down the mountain, he did not know that

his face shone because of his speaking with God. Moses' face reflected the glory of God's presence in His life. The people were afraid to come near him.

"When Moses finished speaking to them, he put a veil over his face. But whenever he entered the Lord's presence to speak with Him, he removed the veil until he came out. And when he came out and told the Israelites what he had been commanded, they saw that his face was radiant. Then Moses would put the veil over his face until he went in to speak with the Lord" (Exodus 34:33-35).

Thankfully, like Moses, when we come to Christ, the veil is removed from our heart, and we are able to come with unveiled faces to Him (2 Corinthians 3:14-16).

Removal of the veil gives us full access to God. We can constantly behold Christ's divine glory, and this beholding transforms us from glory to glory. It makes us more and more like Him as we are changed into His glorious image. There is nothing between you and God.

Your face will shine with the brightness of

His face. So, you are transfigured much like the Messiah, and your life will gradually become brighter and more beautiful. As God enters your life, you will become like Him.

"Those who look to Him for help will be radiant with joy; no shadow of shame will darken their faces" (Psalm 34:5 NLT).

Yes, it takes a deliberate beholding. You and I need to make it a priority to enter this place with God. And when you do, He is able to change your approach, your attitude, your demeanor, and your desires. Because of this, others will be in wonder of your spiritual facelift. For only God can illumine your appearance and soften someone's harsh countenance (Ecclesiastes 8:1).

"The ways of right-living people glow with light; the longer they live, the brighter they shine. But the road of wrongdoing gets darker and darker—travelers can't see a thing; they fall flat on their faces" (Proverbs 4:18 MSG).

Both David and Paul were smitten with the presence of the Lord. They wanted to gaze upon the beauty of the Lord and spend time in

21

His presence. And the more they did, the more He increased in their lives. Just as these great men of the faith were intentional about their time with God, you and I also have to be deliberate with making Him our priority.

What's the *one thing* that your heart craves? What's the *one thing* that you think would change your life? Is it that you seek to dwell in His presence and behold the beauty of the Lord?

Take a Deliberate Step!

As we abide, draw near, and behold God, may we be encouraged by Psalm 5:3. "In the morning, O Lord, You will hear my voice; in the morning I will order my prayer to You and eagerly watch."

Is your voice the first sound the Lord hears? Or is it Google, Facebook, Instagram, or some other form of social media? It's easy to be drawn into the virtual world or a quick read of the book-of-the-month on your table. Distraction can be very subtle and not a bad thing, but the next thing you know, you are fully engulfed in the things of the world rather than seeking Him.

Our priority should be to first seek His Kingdom and His righteousness (Matthew 6:33).

In Deuteronomy 4, Moses warns the Israelites to be watchful and careful to not make idols for themselves that will draw them away from the one true God. However, they do not heed his warnings and serve other gods, "the work of man's hands, wood and stone,

which neither see nor hear, nor eat nor smell. . .
But from there you will seek the Lord your
God, and you will find Him if you search for
Him with all your heart and all your soul"
(Deuteronomy 4:28-29).

Just as the Israelites were sitting in their
disobedience and serving the creation and not
the Creator, you may find yourself in this very
situation—one where you have good intentions,
but you are drawn away by the demands of the
day. Cultural pressure has gotten the best of
you. However, in the midst of your rubble, if
you turn to God and seek Him, He will let you
find Him. He wants nothing more than to be
found by you.

Most of us long to know God deeper and
be known by Him. But you say, "There is so
much that vies for my attention. Where and
how do I make the time to put Jesus first?" You
might start out with good intentions to read a
daily devotion or a Proverb each day, but then
just as the weeks pass by so does your daily
reading, and you forgo your reading time.

God yearns to be your priority.

He waits to hear your voice first thing in the morning. Is your voice what He hears? Ouch!

Yes, the Lord wants to have fellowship with us, but He will not force a relationship upon you. The choice is yours for the taking. It will need to be your daily choice to seek Him and allow His guidance in the quietness of your moments with Him.

If you have allowed the busyness of the day and daily demands of life to invade your space that once was reserved for the Lord, what's next?

Take a deep breath and start over.

It's okay. God has not moved.

In the first chapter of Haggai, Haggai challenges the Israelites to consider their ways—their lifestyle. They were doing a good job of caring for their own homes, but the home of the Lord laid desolate. Haggai then challenged the Israelites to go up to the mountain, bring down the wood, and rebuild the temple. Just as the Israelites were to consider their ways, so are we. Therefore, if God is speaking into your heart to consider your ways, lay down the things that have taken the place of your time with Him and make spending time in His presence your priority.

It's as easy as calling out to Him, abiding with Him, and asking for more of Him.

It is His power within us that allows us to live above circumstances, other's opinions, and our own expectations. You are loved and are a forever thought on His mind.

When your quiet time becomes optional, stress takes charge.

Asaph, while writing Psalm 73, wondered why the wicked prosper. Focusing on the actions of others, he started to take his eyes off God, until one day when he went into the sanctuary of God (Psalm 73:17). This sanctuary place can be described as a consecrated thing, a holy place, a cleansing river, or the secret place. When Asaph entered this sanctuary, God revealed His heart to him. He realized he was becoming bitter (Psalm 73:21). But then Asaph began to remember God's sovereignty and refocused his thoughts on his own life rather than being caught up with the actions of the wicked and in conclusion, Asaph knew the nearness of God was his good. Therefore, he refocused, making the Lord God his refuge so that he could share of God's works (Psalm 73:28).

If you find yourself a little like Asaph, wondering where God is in all of life, or your thoughts are centered on the ways of others, return to the Lord and seek Him that you may live (Amos 5:6), and make Him your main priority. We know that God searches for those of us who fully commit our hearts to Him (2 Chronicles 16:9). Enter into this place of security with God. Seek Him with all your heart and ask Him to become greater in your life as you take the backseat to His divine plan.

Prayer Response

Oh Lord, I bring myself to You and ask You to search my heart. Examine me and know my anxious thoughts, see if there be any hurtful way in me, and lead me back to you (Psalm 139:23-24). Help me to keep You as my daily priority and allow You to have Your way. I hope that others may see the work of Your hands in my life and reflect Your character: love, joy, peace, patience, kindness, goodness, faithfulness, gentleness, and self-control as You increase and I decrease.

Amen

REFLECTIONS TO PONDER. . .

What do you need to do
to make Jesus your priority?

Do you need to create a space
to meet with God regularly?

What will it take for Jesus
to increase in your life?

Have you allowed God access
to your heart?

In what ways does God want
more access to your heart?

CHAPTER TWO

LESS OF ME

"Humble yourselves in the presence
of the Lord, and He will exalt you."

JAMES 4:10

Less of me...

This attitude is somewhat foreign in today's culture. The world screams, "Me, me, me! It's all about me. My happiness. My satisfaction. My achievements."

Yes, it's important to strive for excellence. In fact, God calls us to do the best we can in all we do. However, during the pursuit of excellence, we can easily lose ourselves as the attention, achievement, or success often turn our focus back on ourselves. And sadly, this self-edifying mindset and attitude can be at the expense of others, steamrolling over them to get what we want and where we want to be. The concept that our actions should serve others and the idea that living for someone other than ourselves are both counterintuitive to today's ideals. So, how do you and I live out Philippians 2:3-4 in the *selfie*-centered world we find ourselves living in?

"Do nothing from selfishness or empty conceit, but with humility of mind regard one another as more important than yourselves; do not merely look out for your own personal interests, but also for the interests of others."

Living for others is something we have to be deliberate about. It's not easy. It's not always popular. But, it's how God calls us to walk out our days. Any small act of surrender is an act of love, first to the Lord and second to your fellow man. When you and I surrender to what God asks of us, it takes you beyond yourself.

If anyone had the privilege to elevate or think highly of himself, it was Jesus Christ. He came down from the highest place imaginable— heaven (John 3:13). However, His attitude was one of a humble servant. "For even the Son of Man did not come to be served, but to serve, and to give His life as a ransom for many" (Mark 10:45). His surrender was the highest act of love.

Let's learn a lesson from Philippians 2:5-11.

> "Have this attitude in yourselves which was also in Christ Jesus, who, although He existed in the form of God, did not regard equality with God a thing to be grasped, but emptied Himself, taking the form of a bond-servant, and being made in the likeness of men. Being found in appearance as a man, He humbled Himself by becoming obedient to the point of death, even death on a cross. For this reason also, God highly exalted Him, and bestowed on Him the name which is above every name, so that at the name of Jesus every knee will bow, of those who are in heaven and on earth and under the earth, and that every tongue will confess that Jesus Christ is Lord, to the glory of God the Father."

What Does It Mean to Have Less of Me?

Theology writer, Colin D. Smith writes in his blog, "Jesus was and will always be divine. Prior to the incarnation, Jesus shared in all the divine attributes. However, for God's plan of salvation to come to fruition, it was necessary for Christ to set aside the privileges that came with divine status. He embodied a flesh form and was subject to all that's human: time, hunger, temptation, love, and death. He did not cease being divine, but this was certainly a huge step down, in some way comparable to a king being reduced to a beggar."[3]

Let's face it, having a humble attitude is what it is—humbling! To humble yourself means having or showing a modest or low estimate of your own importance.[4] However, this doesn't mean you shouldn't have a healthy perspective of yourself. No, it's quite the opposite. God desires that we view ourselves positively in light of who He is and Whose we are—chosen, a royal priesthood, a people for God's own possession (1 Peter 2:9).

See, it's because you know the God who provides it all that you will want to serve Him with the fullness of your heart.

Humbling yourself before God will allow Him lordship of your life. He is all-supreme and wants to be the main authority in your life and the master designer of your days. Keep Jesus as the Source of Truth—your True North. As you fix your eyes on Jesus, the author and perfecter of your faith, and abandon yourself to depths of intimacy with Him, you will discover the freedom that only He can supply. He will be the lifter of your head (Psalm 3:3).

PRINCIPLES FOR LESS OF ME

PRINCIPLE #1
Empty Yourself

"Emptied Himself, taking the form of a bond-servant, and being in the likeness of men."

PHILIPPIANS 2:7

Empty yourself and submit your plans to the God who prepared the day beforehand. As you come into His presence, you will experience the depths of God's love for you, and you will begin to allow His plans to become the heartbeat of your existence. As you become captured by the extent and depth of Jesus' love for you, the laying down of your life and surrendering yourself to Jesus will become a little more palatable. Your devotion to follow His lead rather than completing your agenda will take on a new life of its own.

Servanthood is a way of concentrated living—a deliberate decision to allow God to be the one in control. He will be at the center of it all. The way up is down.

A heart of servanthood leads to exaltation and honor.

A heart of surrender leads to purpose, passion, and power. A purpose greater than ourselves. A passion to glorify God and not please man. A power that will allow you to live beyond yourself.

When you allow the Holy Spirit to fill your heart with God's love (Romans 5:5), surrendering to Him becomes attainable.

Once you do this, you will begin to understand His power, which mightily works within you (Ephesians 3:20).

Walk through your days with a prostrate heart completely overcome by His existence in the intricate detail of your being. He's bigger than all your ideas, all your feelings, and all your dreams. Although, at times, you may be unsure of the path you are going down, know He has your best interest at heart, and in His due time He will exalt you. He will lift you up.

The way up is down.

You may be asked to lay down your dreams, desires, or demands of the day. He will not despise the tenderness of your broken and contrite heart as you humbly lay down your self-centeredness at His feet and trust Him to work out His perfect plan for you as you look in the fullness of His goodness and grace. Having a humble attitude is not all in the position of your body, but in the stance of your heart.

If Christ was willing to humble Himself like this, then we Christians, who call ourselves after His name, should display that same kind of humility to one another, not exalting ourselves over each other, but considering the needs of others as more important than our own.

PRINCIPLE #2
Become Obedient

"Being found in appearance as a man, He humbled Himself by becoming obedient to the point of death, even death on a cross."

PHILIPPIANS 2:8

Obedience is surrender to what God wants, not what we desire or think we are entitled to. If I asked you the question, do you want to be a person who is obedient to Christ? You most likely would answer with an emphatic, Yes! But what if I added to the question, to what extent would you be willing to go to be obedient to Christ?

Christ went to the cross. What is He asking you to lay down—your dream, desires, demands, or dependencies?

While working through Priscilla Shirer's Gideon Bible study, I came across this very pertinent question, which came at a pivotal time in my life: "Are you holding onto something God is asking you to release; asking you to lay down?"[5] Wow, this question rocked my early morning time with God. You know, that time in the middle of the night when you can't sleep...2 a.m...and you feel God nudging you to spend time with Him. I wiggled my way out of bed, hit my couch, and began to listen to His still, small voice. I must admit, it is not what you always want to hear, even though you know you are hearing Him loud and clear. What do you do with what you hear? Obedience is what God wants. Obedience shows that you recognize God is in control, and you will trust Him with the outcome. Removing myself from a loved position was not what I wanted, but it is what God desired. Over time, I saw the bigger picture. Stepping away from that role gave God the space to take me outside my current circumstances to serve Him in a new way that I never thought possible. Even if you think the decision being made brings you a little lower than anticipated, trust God knows what He is asking of you—for He knows the plans for your life (Jeremiah 29:11). "Do what He commands you to do" (John 2:5).

Obedience can be a difficult decision, especially when you may not come out smelling like roses.

Obedience can, at times, feel like a death. Either you may feel like you'll die if you don't follow through on what God is asking you to do, or the act of obedience causes a death, of sorts, in a relationship or possibly of your reputation. However, if you don't obey what He is asking of you, you most likely will forfeit His divine peace.

Obedience is the key to a deeper faith and walk with your heavenly Father. Once you experience the peace of God that comes to you because you went to a place with Him that required every living part of your existence, He knows you're willing to trust Him with the outcome, no matter the cost. Yes, obedience is up to you. Outcome is up to God.

Is it hard? Yes, it is!

Are there times you will go to battle with yourself and God? Yes, there are!

Matthew 26:36-39 shows us that even Jesus confronted God regarding His death on the cross.

> **"Then Jesus came with them to a place called Gethsemane, and said to His disciples, 'Sit here while I go over there and pray.' And He took with Him Peter and the two sons of Zebedee, and began to be grieved and distressed. Then He said to them, 'My soul is deeply grieved, to the point of death; remain here and keep watch with Me.' And He went a little beyond them, and fell on His face and prayed, saying, 'My Father, if it is possible, let this cup pass from Me; yet not as I will, but as You will.'"**

Jesus wasn't afraid to ask His Father to reconsider. He approached Him three times with the same question (Matthew 26:44). Although, He was willing to submit and let His Father's will prevail.

In the first part of Matthew 26:39, we see Jesus cry out with raw emotion saying, "My Father, if it is possible, let this cup pass from Me."

First, we see Jesus went beyond the others to a place where it was just Him and His Father.

Second, He fell on His face and prayed—a humble posture and attitude.

Third, there is the little word, if—*if* it is possible. *If* could mean a wishful thought, but one possibly not answered the way you hoped. However, Jesus still asked.

Lastly, although Jesus made His request to God, we see at the end of Matthew 26:39 that He finished His prayer with, "Not My will, but Your will." He would accept the outcome no matter the answer.

Just as Jesus went a little beyond His companions, so must you. One of the greatest things you can do for others is to let them off the hook. Let them stand outside and watch at times. Allow your friends NOT to be at the position of God. Yes, we have to at times—as Jesus went a little beyond with His Father and asked His friends to stay behind and pray—that is what we have to allow for our friends. We have to grant them permission to be on the outside, watching while we do business with

God. Oh, yes, by all means ask them to pray with you and for you. But then there is a time to release them, and enter into your private meeting with your Father. In that secret place with Him, that little beyond abode, He will disclose Himself to you. You will experience the Master's touch, which will allow you to move out with confidence and security. In Luke 22:43, we read the answer to Jesus' request, "Now an angel from heaven appeared to Him, strengthening Him."

Sometimes you will not receive the answer you hoped for, but Jesus will send an angel to strengthen you and the power of the Holy Spirit to fill you up, so that you may be poured out (Romans 15:13).

God Does the Exalting in His Time

**"For this reason also,
God highly exalted Him..."**

PHILIPPIANS 2:9

Are there times you want to take the reins and elevate yourself? Oh, I have tried a time or two, but in the end, God has the final word. Exaltation comes from God. Once we accept this and stop trying to override Him, life will be more acceptable.

James 4:6-10 gives us the equation to triumph over self-centeredness, pride, and the desire to be the Lord of our lives.

> **"But He gives a greater grace. Therefore it says, 'God is opposed to the proud, but gives grace to the humble.' Submit therefore to God. Resist the devil and he will flee from you. Draw near to God and He will draw near to you. Cleanse your hands, you sinners; and**

purify your hearts, you double-minded. Be miserable and mourn and weep; let your laughter be turned into mourning and your joy to gloom. Humble yourselves in the presence of the Lord, and He will exalt you."

The promise of exaltation comes when you and I submit to God, resist the devil, draw near to God, and purify our hearts in the presence of the Lord. Submit, resist, draw near, and purify are active verbs that make a difference in defending our hearts against self-exaltation. If you continually refresh your mind with the following steps, you will be more likely to humble yourself:

1. Commit your ways to God
2. Come close to Him
3. Cleanse your heart of impurities
4. Confess your sins to Him

My pastor once put it like this: *Give In, Get Close, Clean Up, and Get Down.*

May God help us to trust His plan regardless of His reply—yes, no, or wait.

Indeed, as His Word reminds us, "For as the heavens are higher than the earth, so are My ways higher than your ways and My thoughts than your thoughts" (Isaiah 55:9).

God knows the beginning to the end of your life, and what it will take to make you more like His Son. Embrace the sovereignty of God and allow Him to have His way. If the Son of Man did not come to be served, but rather to serve (Matthew 20:28), shouldn't you and I have the same attitude?

Take a Deliberate Step!

As I close out this chapter, I would be remiss not to share one of the greatest examples of what it looks like to empty ourselves, become obedient, and accept exultation in God's time. John 13:1-5 (NLT) shares a beautiful illustration through the life of Jesus.

> "Before the Passover celebration, Jesus knew that His hour had come to leave this world and return to His Father. He had loved His disciples during His ministry on earth, and now He loved them to the very end. It was time for supper, and the devil had already prompted Judas, son of Simon Iscariot, to betray Jesus. Jesus knew that the Father had given Him authority over everything and that He had come from God and would return to God. So He got up from the table, took off His robe, wrapped a towel around His waist, and poured water into a basin. Then He began to wash the disciples' feet, drying them with the towel He had around Him."

The lesson Jesus was teaching involves the importance of serving one another in humility of heart and becoming a servant leader. Normally a servant performed the lowly task of washing the guests' feet, but Jesus wanted to fulfill Mark 10:45, "For even the Son of Man did not come to be served, but to serve, and to give His life a ransom for many."[6] This was a critically important lesson the disciples had been slow to learn. Jesus washing their feet was an extraordinarily effective way of making the point that it's not all about you, rather it's about showing the love of God to your fellow man. Also, Jesus was fully aware that Judas Iscariot would betray Him and Peter would deny Him. Putting all that aside, Jesus still bent down, washed their feet, and gently wiped them off. His love for His disciples was displayed in and through a towel. This was not just any ole' towel laying amongst them, but one that was wrapped around Jesus' very own waist.

This beautiful act of love and service was followed by a command in John 13:14-15. "You call Me Teacher and Lord; and you are right, for so I am. If I then, the Lord and the Teacher, washed your feet, you also ought to wash one another's feet. For I gave you an example that you also should do as I did to you."

This command is not just for the disciples who walked the dusty roads with Jesus. We have the same command—serve each other with love and respect. Remember any small act of surrender is an act of love.

Let us take the principles shared in this chapter and live an abundant life fully committed to Him through our acts of service, love, forgiveness, and humility as displayed by the One who deserves all our praise.

May He continue to become greater as you become less.

Prayer Response

Oh Lord, never allow me to think
that some tasks are beneath
my dignity or too insignificant for
me to do. May I always have a
humble approach to the things You
ask me to do with a heart of pure
surrender as You increase in
every aspect of my life.

Amen

REFLECTIONS TO PONDER...

What is God asking you
to surrender to Him?

Are you doing anything
out of selfish ambition?

Is there something you are
holding onto that God
is asking you to release to Him?

Principles for Fruitful Living

"Now to Him who is able to do far more abundantly beyond all that we ask or think, according to the power that works within us, to Him be the glory in the church and in Christ Jesus to all generations forever and ever. Amen."

EPHESIANS 3:20-21

You and I want our lives to matter, to leave our marks on this generation and the next. We want to live abundant lives, which are empowered by the Holy Spirit. However, before you can produce anything, you must first be connected to the main source who does the increasing. In the Gospel of John,

Jesus speaks of Himself as the vine, which is actually His last "I am" statement recorded in Scripture: I am the true vine (John 15:1).

The *true* vine in the vineyard is the essential trunk of the vine, and on the vine are many branches. Some branches are productive, while others produce little to no fruit. This imagery portrays Jesus as the main trunk and you and I as the branches. Separate from Him, you are unable to produce lasting fruit. He is the source of all your life and every good thing you do. Without this connection, you are incapable of living an empowered and fruitful life. Apart from Him, you can do nothing. Power comes from the Vine—not from the branches. To live a purposeful, fruitful, and empowered life, you must be rooted in the depths of God.

As we have already established, you will want to spend concentrated time with the Lord in the stillness of your day. When you make Him your main delight, He will multiply your effort. He made you full of great potential and purpose. He made you to be fruitful, producing only what brings Him glory. Too many times, we rush through the abiding process and charge ahead to the end product, all the while wondering why things aren't working for our good.

Because you have been made ALIVE with Jesus (Colossians 2:13), together you can accomplish great things and live fruitful lives! Yes, you and I want our lives to matter. We want to tell the next generation the praises of the Lord, His strength, and the wondrous works He has done (Psalm 78:4)!

God has kept you alive and given you opportunity for fruitful living. Yes, fruitful living!

Although, there may be mornings you feel slightly sluggish, God is in the business of breathing breath into your lungs, so that you may come ALIVE and know that He is the Lord (Ezekiel 37:6).

Psalm 1:2-3 (NLT) gives you purposeful components to abundant living, "But they delight in the law of the Lord, meditating on it day and night. They are like trees planted along the riverbank, bearing fruit each season.

Their leaves never wither, and they prosper in all they do."

This Scripture calls us to delight in the Lord, meditate on His Word, and grow deep roots in Him. If you establish these disciplines and embed yourself with these qualities, it will help you find peace in God's will for your life and a power that only comes from the Living Water. In John 7:38, we see Jesus speaking with the crowds sharing how the "living water" is the Holy Spirit whom they will receive upon belief in Him after His ascension to heaven. "Anyone who believes in Me may come and drink! For the Scriptures declare, 'Rivers of living water will flow from his heart.'"

You and I have a power greater than our natural strength. All we need to do is tap into that power and watch God show off. We will have a spiritual caffeine explosion when we allow the Spirit's work in our lives.

PRINCIPLES FOR ACHIEVING A FRUITFUL LIFE

PRINCIPLE #1
Receive God's Pruning

"Every branch in Me that does not bear fruit, He takes away; and every branch that bears fruit, He prunes so that it may bear more fruit."

JOHN 15:2

Just as there is the promise of fruitfulness, there is the promise of pruning. John 15:2 says, "Every branch in Me that does not bear fruit, He takes away; and every branch that bears fruit, He prunes so that it may bear more fruit." Yes, there will be times the Gardener (God) clips you for greater use. If you feel that God has cut away things from your life, most likely He wants your connection to Him to be stronger. And through the seclusion, you will discover things about yourself and God that you may not have known without the pruning. Your solitude with God will test your commitment to Him, awaken the awareness of self-satisfaction, and the importance of relationships—your relationship with God and with others. Consider Paul. He penned many of his letters to the New Testament believers while under house arrest. There is no telling what God will reveal to you while sequestered from others.

If you're growing back from His clipping, don't resist the process. Instead embrace it and thank Him for caring enough to take the time to cultivate your life. Remember, the Gardner only prunes branches that belong to Him so that they may bear more fruit. So, if you feel disconnected, return to the Vine, reconnect with the Lord, and rely on Him to produce a greater harvest. He chose you and commissioned you to go and bear fruit that would remain (John 15:16). Every gardener knows the pruning process brings forth greater quantity and quality of fruit. Your connection to the Vine becomes sweeter the more you welcome His discipline, correction, and love. It is all to accomplish a more fruit bearing life—one that brings honor to your Father and proves you are His disciple. The progression of a follower of Christ will be to bear fruit, more fruit, then much fruit (John 15:8).

PRINCIPLE #2

Practice Righteousness

"Let the one who does wrong, still do wrong;
and the one who is filthy, still be filthy;
and let the one who is righteous,
still practice righteousness; and the one
who is holy, still keep himself holy."

REVELATION 22:11

Let us learn this lesson from Psalm 92:12-15:

> "The righteous man will flourish like the palm tree, he will grow like a cedar in Lebanon.

> Planted in the house of the Lord, they will flourish in the courts of our God.

> They will still yield fruit in old age; they shall be full of sap and very green,

> To declare that the Lord is upright; He is my rock, and there is no unrighteousness in Him."

These verses are a beautiful picture of a person who has willfully and sincerely repented of their sins, accepted the Lord Jesus as their personal Savior, and in turn wears the label of *righteous and godly*. This seems like a high and lofty label to wear, but your loving Father pins it on you when you come desiring to live a life fully devoted to Him and express a continual desire to practice righteousness.

Thankfully, He restores your soul and guides you in the paths of His righteousness for His name's sake (Psalm 23:3). God promises that a righteous life will flourish and grow. "For the eyes of the Lord move to and fro throughout the earth that He may strongly support those whose heart is completely His" (2 Chronicles 16:9a).

God's desire is that you will move into a wholehearted lifestyle—one devoted fully to Him, producing much fruit. Once you devote yourself totally to Him, there are no boundaries to how He will use you for His glory.

We can learn volumes from the beautiful illustration of the palm tree and the cedar in

Lebanon. As depicted in Psalm 92, they bear much fruit. Specifically, palm trees grow deep roots into the ground until they strike living springs. Then they display a towering beauty. When strong winds come, the root system of the palm tree is not weakened. It's actually strengthened by these storms! May you grow deep roots in Christ, drawing nourishment for your daily living, and be able to live above your circumstances with a towering beauty for others to see the strength of the Lord. Having a secure root system in place will help you to survive the storms.

Along the same lines, cedar trees are strong and mighty with an unwavering strength. May you bear the strength of a cedar as you call upon the name of the Lord for your power. Your flourishing and growth will continue into old age as you seek God for nourishment and might.

And, oh, that you and I would pay careful attention to the words King Solomon spoke in 1 Kings 8:61, "Let your hearts be wholly devoted to the Lord our God, to walk in His statutes and to keep His commandments, as at this day."

PRINCIPLE # 3
Embrace the Wait

"He gives strength to the weary, and to him who lacks might He increases power. Though youths grow weary and tired, and vigorous young men stumble badly, yet those who wait for the Lord will gain new strength; they will mount up with wings like eagles, they will run and not get tired, they will walk and not become weary."

ISAIAH 40:29-31

Wait. That isn't a word many of us like or, for that matter, even accept. Many times, we run ahead of God when He has asked us to wait, and we quickly learn that hindsight is 20/20 vision. You have likely heard the saying: "For such a time as this." The verse before us states that those who wait upon the Lord will renew their strength. In due time, my friend, in due time.

But you want it *now*.

What happens in the wait can drive you closer to the heart of God and deeper into His Word. The deeper you go, the clearer His will becomes to you. I am not going to sugarcoat it—waiting is hard.

Are there days when you feel powerless and as though you are running on empty? Do you experience days you want to crawl back into bed and pull the covers over your head? It's normal at times to feel this way. Yes, you will have days like this. When you feel this way, you need to tap into a strength and power beyond yourself—God's strength. He will secure you with His strength (Psalm 18:32).

Too many times, we try to manipulate situations. At times, we even try to convince God of our plans. His Word tells us our times are in His hands (Psalm 31:15) and "...even before we were born, God planned in advance our destiny and the good works we would do to fulfill it" (Ephesians 2:10 TPT). Therefore, what you will need to do is walk in His plans for you. God invites you to claim His promise of power as He gives strength to the weary by increasing their power. Just as God deepens your relationship with Him through times of waiting, He also increases your energy, faith, endurance, and strength. Waiting is hard, but as you embrace the wait, what you learn can be the catalyst of His future design. He molds you into the fullness of your destiny and will take you to depths of trust beyond your own understanding. "Delight yourself in the Lord; and He will give you the desires of your heart. Commit your way to the Lord, trust also in Him, and He will do it" (Psalm 37:4-5).

Surely, waiting on Him is never wasted time! The wings where you seek refuge (Psalm 91:4) can be the same wings you soar on. Bring your weariness, your aching heart, and your insipidness to the Giver of strength, power, and vitality. Allow Him to rejuvenate your tired soul.

Every single day, you have the greatest Mediator working on your behalf. Even when things seem to go wrong and you feel powerless, He's making sure that everything works according to His purpose. His strength will carry you according to His power, which mightily works within you (Colossians 1:29). God is not selfish about His power. Rather, He is abundantly generous, sharing His power with you and inviting you to partake in it. Set out to be empowered by God as He recharges, refuels, and renews both your body and soul. (Isaiah 11:2 NLT).

- Empowered to grow in your faith
- Empowered to share the love of Jesus
- Empowered to serve others better
- Empowered to take that step in faith where God is calling you to go

Take a Deliberate Step!

Receiving God's pruning, practicing righteous-ness, and embracing the wait are not easy principles to apply, but we know that God offers a strength beyond ourselves to achieve such things through the Holy Spirit. Will you choose to tap into His power and live your life to its fullest potential? Or, are you going to settle for ease and comfort? What you do with the opportunities given to you is your gift back to God through your response, action, and commitment. You must continue to move forward. For, "whatever your hand finds to do, do it with all your might," (Ecclesiastes 9:10a) and flourish right where you are planted.

Fruitful living will require purposeful steps to accomplish all that God has for you. What do you and I need to do to live in the hundred-fold, our fullest potential? Below are six ways we can pursue fruitful living and unlock the power to step out in faith.

1. **Receive, believe, achieve.** Hear the Word of God daily, believe it, and then take action.

> "But one who looks intently at the perfect law, the law of liberty, and abides by it, not having become a forgetful hearer but an effectual doer, this man will be blessed in what he does."
> JAMES 1:25

2. **Move beyond the past.** Don't allow past attempts, failures, or fears to stop you from moving forward.

> "Once you were dead because of your disobedience and your many sins. You used to live in sin. . . All of us used to live that way, following the passionate desires and inclinations of our sinful nature. By our very nature we were subject to God's anger, just like everyone else. But God is so rich in mercy, and he loved us so much, that even though we were dead because of our sins, he gave us life when he raised Christ from the dead."
> EPHESIANS 2:1-5 NLT

3. **Be a goal-setter and a goal-keeper.** As God reveals His plan for you, make a list of what you want to accomplish, and then set deadlines. Be specific. Yes, God calls us to make plans and create deadlines, but it's important for you to be flexible when He steps in to nudge you in your direction.

> "The plans of the heart belong to man,
> but the answer of the tongue is from the Lord.
> The heart of man plans his way, but
> the Lord establishes his steps."
> PROVERBS 16:1 (NASB), 9 (ESV)

4. **Know your why.** Know why you are doing what you are doing and be emotionally connected to the action. Always check the motive as to why you do the things you're pursuing.

> "Commit your way to the Lord,
> trust also in Him, and He will do it."
> PSALM 37:5

5. **Trust God with the outcome.** Do your part as God leads, and then allow Him to complete

it. Yes, following Jesus means relinquishing control and allowing Him to take the wheel. He will reveal all that you need to know for each step. As we trust Him with the outcome, may our prayer be that He would give us the wisdom to search His plans as we walk in His ways.

"For we are His workmanship, created in Christ Jesus for good works, which God prepared beforehand so that we would walk in them."

EPHESIANS 2:10

"For I know the plans I have for you, declares the Lord, plans for welfare and not for evil, to give you a future and a hope."

JEREMIAH 29:11 ESV

6. **Make the move.** Pray, pray, pray, and then take the step of faith needed to accomplish all God is calling you to. Neale Donald Walsch, author of *Conversations with God*, says,"Life begins at the end of your comfort zone."

"Consecrate yourselves, for tomorrow the Lord will do wonders among you."

JOSHUA 3:5

"But you should keep a clear mind
in every situation. Don't be afraid of suffering
for the Lord. Work at telling others
the Good News, and fully carry out the
ministry God has given you."
2 Timothy 4:5

It is said of Oswald Chambers, author of
My Utmost for His Highest devotional, that he
was a man who was "never content with low
achievements...always climbing the mountain
peaks."

I once read the story of a man who died
while climbing one of the highest peaks of the
Alps. "He died climbing" are the words etched
upon his gravestone.

That story, along with Oswald Chambers'
perseverance, had a huge impact on my life—
one I haven't forgotten. Do you and I have this
same attitude? It's one that, "whatever you do,
you do with excellence" (Ecclesiastes 9:10).
Or, are there times you have a "just get by"
mentality? As children of God, we are called to
a higher standard of living beyond ourselves.

All He asks from us is to come to Him with what we have, and trust Him with the outcome. He will do the multiplying.

In Matthew 25:1-13, we read the Parable of the Ten Virgins. There were five prudent virgins and five foolish virgins. The five prudent virgins were found ready for the arrival of the bridegroom, whereas the foolish virgins were not prepared and wanted to borrow the oil from the five wise ladies. They had a "just get by" mentality. They were not found ready. When they realized their lack, it was too late.

In the next parable, Matthew 25:14-30, we read about the Talents. The first man who was given five talents, doubled his talents; the second man who was given two talents also doubled his talents; the last man was given only one talent, but he hid it out of fear. The first two men were blessed. The last man's talent was taken away and dispersed between the other two men.

Both of these parables illustrate the value of being watchful, prepared, and faithful with what has been given to us. I want to be among the five virgins and two men. I want to be prudent and wise.

God is not going to wave a magic wand and make all of your desires and dreams come true. He wants you to:

- Commit your ways to Him (Psalm 37:5)
- Practice the gift He has given you (1 Timothy 4:15)
- Be found faithful to the calling He has blessed you with (Ephesians 4:1)

When you commit your way to Him and allow Him to determine the time and place of blessing, you will watch Him go above and beyond what you could ever imagine or think according to the power working within you (Ephesians 3:20).

The power working within you from Ephesians 3:20 is the Holy Spirit's power. Yes, you already have this power if you have received Jesus' love in your heart and confessed Him as Lord! You just have to tap into His power and step out in faith. Your one act of obedience may impact the people who walk with you, and also a generation that follows.

As I conclude, More of Him Ministries celebrates 10 years of ministry. As I reflect on these years, I stand amazed at all God has done in me personally, building a stronger faith, trust, and reliance on Him. Yet, He gave me a strength beyond myself to make a move, take a chance, and trust Him with each step.

If you are like me, you may think to yourself, *But I have never gone this way before.* It's okay. Just don't let those thoughts paralyze you and stop you from experiencing all God has for you. Søren Kierkegaard, a Danish philosopher, theologian, poet, social critic, and religious author, said it best when he wrote, "Life can only be understood backwards, but it must be lived forwards."

Others may try to hold you back, but obey the voice of God and do not listen to the discouragement of man. Nothing others do or say should ever upset the one whose life is built upon God as the foundation. Remember this—God is for you (Psalm 56:9b). You must continue to move forward despite not being applauded and supported by those you think should be cheering you on.

Is there something God is calling you to do? Do you feel Him tugging on your heartstrings to pass something on to that person you have been reluctant to talk with? Maybe you desire to take the leap into full-time ministry, open a coffee shop, take a painting class, or make a job change?

Time is fleeting! *Now* is the time. He is empowering you to live beyond yourself. Trust Him to fuel your desires with His strength.

Make the move. Take the leap.

Theodore Roosevelt said, "Believe you can, and you're halfway there." Belief comes from a deep confidence that you have heard from God. Then, you must allow God to advance the second half. Remember: Obedience is up to you. Outcome is up to God.

He has your useful, upright, and honorable works planned out according to His perfect design. All you need to do is walk in them. Walk in the way He leads you. When you make a conscious effort to rely on God and not yourself, things begin to change.

He is empowering you to live your best life. Live it in His strength, and His plans will be accomplished. Fruitful living is only accomplished when you stay connected to Jesus and allow Him to direct your steps.

Prayer Response

Oh Lord, thank You for Your love
and the strength You empower
me with. If I don't have You, I don't
have anything. You are my life!
Help me to desire You above everything and continually abide in Your
presence for needed strength.
Go before me and prepare the way
that I may walk in it.

Amen

REFLECTIONS TO PONDER...

Is your connection to the Vine strong?
If not, what will you need to do
to strengthen your connection?

Do you embrace the pruning stage
as being loved by God?

How has the pruning process
drawn you closer to Him?

How is God calling you to a fruitful life?

What step will you take to fulfill
all God has for you?

CHRIST IN YOUR HEART

Have you read this book and wondered how you can have more of Jesus? Maybe you have not yet asked Jesus to be Lord and Savior of your life.

When I was searching and someone mentioned "born again" to me, my first thought was, *What is this? This seems a little radical to me.* Then she explained, and I understood. In the Book of John, Jesus has a conversation with a man named Nicodemus who approached Him curious about the Kingdom of God. Jesus told Nicodemus, "I tell you the truth, unless you are born again, you cannot see the Kingdom of God" (John 3:3 NLT). In the next verse, Nicodemus responded, "How can an old man go back into his mother's womb and be born again?" (John 3:4 NLT)

As a respected leader in the Jewish community, Nicodemus was a moral man who obeyed God's law. Even though he was a fine man, something was missing.

Is something missing in your life? Does your heart feel like there is a hole in it?

Today, just like in the days of Nicodemus, many people confuse "being good" with a "born-again" experience. New birth begins when the Holy Spirit convicts a person of sin. Because of the fall of man, we are spiritually dead and need a Savior. God loved us so much that He provided a spiritual rebirth. All we have to do is ask Him for it. God's Word tells us that we are all sinners (Romans 3:23). Jesus died on a cross and was raised from the dead to save sinners (Colossians 1:20), and if we believe in the Lord Jesus, Scripture assures us we will be saved (Acts 16:31). Colossians 1:22 tells us that He has reconciled us by Christ's physical body through death to present us holy in His sight, without blemish and free from accusation. When we accept Jesus into our hearts and become born anew, we admit that we are sinful and tell God that we want to turn from our sinful ways (Acts 3:19). In this act of faith, Scripture tells us that we are rescued from all evil and given eternal life with God through Jesus' act on the cross where our sins are forgiven (Colossians 1:13-14).

Jesus told Nicodemus that every person who believes in Christ will experience eternal life with Him beyond their human death (John 3:16). We know that Jesus is the way, the truth, and the life. He is the only way we have access to God (John 14:6). To believe in Jesus is to be "born again."

Take this moment to confess your sins and ask Jesus to save you, and the Holy Spirit will come right away to live in your heart. Please don't put this important decision off. "For anyone who calls on the name of the Lord will be saved" (Acts 2:21).

Upon receiving Jesus Christ as your Savior, share this important decision with another person—maybe your pastor, spouse, or a dear friend. I pray that you will find a Bible-believing church to attend so you can continue to worship God, grow in Christ, and serve in the Spirit.

Dear friend, this is a day to rejoice and be happy. As He increases in your life, you will begin to decrease.

Congratulations!

Endnotes

1. James Strong, *The New Strong's Exhaustive Concordance of the Bible*; John Walvoord and Roy Zuck, The Bible Knowledge Commentary: New Testament (Colorado Springs: Cook Communications Ministries, 1983, 2000), 671.

2. *Secrets of the Secret Place*, Bob Sorge, 2001, Oasis House P.O. Box 127, Greenwood, Missouri 64034-0127. 4-5.

3. Smith, Colin D. "Sunday Devotional: Philippians 2:5-11." *Colin D Smith*, 11 Feb. 2012, www.colindsmith.com/blog/2012/02/12/sunday-devotional-philippians-25-11.

4. New Oxford American Dictionary (Second Edition).

5. Shirer, Priscilla. Gideon: LifeWay Press. 2013.

6. "John 13:3-11." *Ryrie Study Bible: New American Standard Bible*, by Charles Caldwell Ryrie, Moody Publishers, 2012. 1707.

ABOUT THE AUTHOR

Jessie Seneca is a national speaker, author, leadership trainer, and founder of More of Him Ministries and SHE Leads Conference. She has a passion to help women experience God's Word for themselves as she encourages them to move into a life fully devoted to God.

Jessie and her husband, John, live in Pennsylvania. They have two adult daughters and wonderful sons-in-law.

Most days you will find Jessie walking her two golden doodles, Bella and Murphy, and enjoying her role as Mimi.

CPSIA information can be obtained
at www.ICGtesting.com
Printed in the USA
LVHW041111010920
664636LV00005B/448